Strange But True Facts of the Civil War

by

Patrick M. Reynolds

Taylor Trade Publishing

Lanham • New York • Boulder • Toronto • Plymouth, UK

Published by Taylor Trade Publishing

An imprint of The Rowman & Littlefield Publishing Group, Inc.

4501 Forbes Boulevard, Suite 200, Lanham, Maryland 20706

Distributed by national book network

Library of Congress Cataloging-in-Publication Data

Reynolds, Patrick M.

Strange but true facts of the Civil War / Patrick M. Reynolds. — 1st Taylor Trade Pub. ed.

p. cm.

Includes bibliographical references and index.

ISBN-13: 978-1-58979-362-0 (pbk. : alk. paper)

ISBN-10: 1-58979-362-5 (pbk. : alk. paper)

1. United States—History—Civil War, 1861–1865—Miscellanea. I. Title.

E468.9.R49 2007

973.7—dc22

2007014404

The paper used in this publication meets the minimum requirements of American National Standard for Information Sciences—Permanence of Paper for Printed Library Materials, ANSI/NISO Z39.48–1992.

Manufactured in the United States of America.

Contents

To
my grandson
Avery Reynolds

Introduction

Aside from the grand and sweeping battles, the great and less-than-adequate leaders, and the famous and lesser-known heroes, the Civil War featured incidents, inventions, and characters that were either unusual, funny, raucous, remarkable, idiotic, oddly coincidental, or just plain weird. This book not only tells their stories, but shows what they looked like.

There are enough strange but true facts about the Civil War to fill volumes, but I have chosen a few topics that do not usually appear in history books, such as the unique weapons that were seen for the first time; women who received distinctive accolades for their service on and off the battlefield; free blacks and slaves who served in the Confederate army; Confederate money and postage stamps; unlikely spies; lost gold; action in the western territories and Mexico; and Confederate raids on northern cities. Did you know that long before 9-11, the Confederates tried to destroy New York City?

This book is a departure from other histories inasmuch as it is fully illustrated, not with period photos and drawings, but with my own tightly rendered watercolors. Thus, my research for this book required as much time to glean the facts as well as find out what the individuals, equipment, weapons, uniforms, and locales looked like.

For over thirty years I have been writing and illustrating a series of special features highlighting *histories your history teacher never heard of*. These features appeared in newspapers across the country. One time, I did an episode titled "Civil War Trivia" for my *Pennsylvania Profiles* illustrated series. On seeing the finished story a friend of mine from Georgia remarked, "There's nothing trivial about the *War of Northern Aggression*." So it goes with this book, there is nothing trivial in it, but there are a lot of Strange But True Facts of the Civil War.

Patrick M. Reynolds

The Republican Party stood for the exclusion of slavery in the western territories, but allowed slavery in the South. Their candidate **Abraham Lincoln** was elected president in November 1860. Southerners were furious and viewed the President-elect as...

a baboon, a wild man from nowhere and a daring and reckless leader of the abolitionists.

Lincoln's election means the freeing of slaves and slave uprisings throughout the South.

SECESSION

Now that a Republican president had been elected, many powerful politicians in the South no longer felt bound to stay in the Union. Between Lincoln's election in November 1860 and his inauguration in March 1861, **seven states** in the deep South **seceded.** Amid parades and much hoopla they formed the **Confederate States of America.** After the war started in April 1861, four more states seceded.

STATES' RIGHTS

Caught in the middle was lame-duck President **James Buchanan** who said in his last State-of-the-Union speech,

*The southern states have **no right** to secede, but Congress has **no power** to make them stay. I only want to keep peace until President Lincoln takes over.*

Lincoln had his own ideas for preserving the Union, but he needed to drum up support. To do this he left home in Springfield, Illinois, for his inauguration in Washington on February 11, 1861, on a strenuous 12-day rail trip of speeches and meetings through the northern industrial states. Meanwhile, a plot was brewing.

BUFFALO · UTICA · SCHENECTADY
SYRACUSE · ALBANY
NEW YORK
CONN.
ILLINOIS
SPRINGFIELD · INDIANA · CLEVELAND
OHIO · PENNSYLVANIA
PITTSBURGH · HARRISBURG · N.J. · NEW YORK
COLUMBUS · LANCASTER · TRENTON
INDIANAPOLIS · PHILADELPHIA
CINCINNATI · MD.
BALTIMORE · MD. · WASHINGTON

1

The Baltimore Plot

In January 1861, on the eve of the Civil War, **Pinkerton detectives** were investigating the possibility of southern secessionists **sabotaging railroad tracks and bridges** in Maryland.

Some of the Pinkertons infiltrated secessionist gangs and learned about a plot that was instigated by the Baltimore **Chief of Police**.

President-elect Lincoln is slated to change trains in Baltimore on the way to his inauguration in Washington.

As Lincoln steps off the train a fight will erupt in the station.

This will divert everyone's attention.

The chief allotted only eight cops to guard Lincoln. They would run to the melee.

Immediately a team of assassins would move in for the kill.

Allan Pinkerton reported the plot to Lincoln, but Abe refused to change his travel plans without further proof.

Since no cop south of the Mason-Dixon Line could be trusted, a federal big-wig turned to the **New York City police.**

At a meeting in January 1861 in Washington **John Kennedy** (center), Superintendent of the New York Police, and his Chief of Detectives George Walling, agreed to investigate the plot.

Kennedy returned to New York and summoned two of his best detectives, W. T. DeVoe and Thomas Sampson. He ordered them to go to Baltimore and obtain confirmation that there was indeed a plot to assassinate President-elect Lincoln.

3

Sampson, calling himself *Anderson from Augusta, Georgia*, and DeVoe, dubbed *Davis from Mobile, Alabama*, went to Baltimore posing as southern gentlemen, and began to hang out with secessionists.

They even joined a military unit called the *Southern Volunteers*, commanded by a flamboyant Texan named Captain Hay.

One day DeVoe received a letter from his wife. It was addressed to his phony name but one of the *Volunteers* happened to see it.

Questioned about getting a letter postmarked *New York*, DeVoe made up an explanation that was almost believable.

The detectives knew that they were now under suspicion and a telegraph to Augusta or Mobile would really blow their cover. It was time to leave.

4

They hopped the first train out of town.

Unfortunately it was heading south—to Washington, DC.

In the capitol they checked into Willard's Hotel under Anderson and Davis. Later that day they came down to the lobby and spotted some Volunteers checking the hotel register.

The undercover cops tried to elude their southern pursuers by mingling with the crowd in the hotel.

Luckily they ran into Tim Webster, a Pinkerton detective working undercover as a secessionist.

Webster escorted them out of town and put them on a northbound train.

But the secessionists were covering all the trains; DeVoe and Sampson were surrounded again.

Somewhere between Washington and Baltimore they jumped off the train.

DeVoe and Sampson made their way back to New York and reported to Superintendent John Kennedy, but it is uncertain if they ever learned anything about a plot to kill Lincoln.

Meanwhile Pinkerton detectives had amassed enough evidence to convince the president-elect to change his travel plans. Lincoln arrived in Harrisburg, Pennsylvania, on February 22, 1861.

He addressed the state legislature while outside the capitol southern spies and sympathizers waited. At 5 p.m. Lincoln joined the governor at a reception/dinner.

Governor Curtin, I must confide in you. There's a plot to assassinate me. My schedule has been changed and I must leave now for Washington.

At 6 p.m., feigning illness, Lincoln left the reception and was driven to a railroad siding outside of Harrisburg where he boarded a regularly scheduled train to Philadelphia. Lincoln made known his dissatisfaction with the situation.

> This cowardly display is wrong. At this critical moment we should show our strength.

Pinkerton's men cut the telegraph wires to keep the rebels from contacting their cohorts.

In Philadelphia Lincoln changed trains and rode with one of Pinkerton's best operatives, a woman named **Kate Warne.** *

Arriving in Baltimore at 3 a.m., Lincoln's coach was uncoupled and pulled through the streets because locomotives were not allowed to go into the city.

Throughout the trip **Kate Warne,** disguised as "Mr. Lincoln's **invalid brother,"** took charge of the security, arranged the railcars and coordinated transportation. Lincoln arrived safely in Washington on the morning of February 23 and was inaugurated nine days later.

The Baltimore Plot was never investigated. Allan Pinkerton, owner of the Chicago-based detective agency which uncovered the plot, kept quiet about it until 1868. On the other hand, John Kennedy craved the glory.

In 1866 he wrote to a historian and claimed all the credit for saving Lincoln's life.

*Special footnote—
Kate Warne's career was cut short by illness. She died in 1868 at the age of 35 and was buried in the Pinkerton family plot in Graceland Cemetery in Chicago, Illinois. She left no family of her own and it was never determined if **Kate Warne** was her real name.

7

Lincoln and the Pirates

Throughout history a pirate was someone who committed violence or robbery on the high seas **without** sanctions from a political authority. If a pirate was captured, he or she was usually hanged.

From the outset of the Civil War, the Union blockaded southern ports. The South's survival depended on international trade, so the Confederate government commissioned **blockade runners.** Sometimes the U.S. Navy captured a blockade runner.

Therefore, in the realm of international law, the southern blockade runners were **legal.** President Lincoln, himself a lawyer, declared,

Captured blockade runners, even though licensed by the Confederate government, shall not be treated as prisoners of war, but as **pirates**!

In early June 1861 blockade runner Thomas Baker and his twelve crewmen of the privateer *Savannah* surrendered to the U.S.S. *Perry*.

They were put on trial at the U.S. Circuit Court in New York City. It ended in a hung jury.

Afterwards, one jury member commented,

Why would a rebel captured on land become a prisoner of war while another reb' captured on water be charged with piracy?

The powers-that-be in Richmond responded.

We're holding a federal hostage for each southern sailor who faces the death penalty.

With that, Lincoln relented.

Nevertheless, throughout the war Lincoln and his top aides referred to Confederate sailors as pirates.

9

EMANCIPATION

Early afternoon, January 1st, 1863–As President Lincoln was about to sign the Emancipation Proclamation, his hand shook so much that he dropped the pen.

He picked it up and slowly signed the document. What was the cause of that affliction?

That morning Lincoln hosted a New Year's reception, a tradition that was started by John Adams in 1801. Lincoln had shaken hundreds of hands and his right hand was left virtually **paralyzed.**

The Emancipation Proclamation was a **political tactic.** By signing the document, Lincoln gained the support of England and France in the war.

The Emancipation Proclamation also satisfied the abolitionists and enabled the Union military to **enlist** 130,000 **African American** soldiers and sailors.

The only slaves that were freed by the Emancipation Proclamation were in the Confederate states where Lincoln had **no** authority. Slaves were **not** freed in the states that stayed in the Union: Maryland, Kentucky, Missouri, and Delaware.

It took the Union winning the war followed by the passage in 1865 of the **13th Amendment** to the Constitution of the United States to **free all** the slaves in the U.S.

On the eve of the Civil War, President Lincoln offered Colonel **Robert E. Lee** command of the Union army. In that capacity, Lee felt that he would eventually be ordered to invade his home state of Virginia, so he politely turned down the president's offer. When Virginia seceded a few days later, Lee was made a general in the Confederate Army and the U.S. government promptly seized his property in **Arlington, Virginia.** The U.S. War Department opened the Arlington National Cemetery on his land in 1864.

But, a year earlier, another section of the general's estate became what is probably the U.S. government's **first major housing project.**

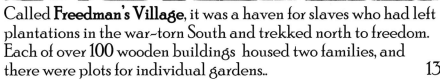

Called **Freedman's Village**, it was a haven for slaves who had left plantations in the war-torn South and trekked north to freedom. Each of over 100 wooden buildings housed two families, and there were plots for individual gardens..

13

Tall Target

Only one Civil War battle took place within Washington, DC.

Confederate Major General Jubal Early attacked Fort Stevens July 11, 1864. The next day President Lincoln, his wife, and Secretary of War Stanton rode out to watch the battle. Lincoln stood on a parapet as a medical officer standing next to him was shot.

An officer urged Lincoln to take cover. This had entered American folklore as the officer yelling,

GET DOWN, YOU FOOL!

When Early observed the imposing fort with 17 cannons, he paused to rest and regroup his troops. This gave General McCook time to reinforce the fort.

That officer was Captain **Oliver Wendell Holmes.** In 1902 President Theodore Roosevelt appointed Holmes to the **Supreme Court** of the United States.

That afternoon, a Union brigade moved out of the fort to engage the Confederates.

At 10 p.m. Early withdrew back to Virginia under the cover of darkness.

UNIQUE WEAPONS

The Peninsular Campaign was General George McClellan's plan to capture the Confederate capital, Richmond, by sailing south, then marching up the peninsula between the James and York rivers in April 1862. The strategy failed and the war dragged on for three more years

A few Union regiments used the new **Ager Gun** popularly called the *Coffee Mill* because bullets were loaded into a hopper that resembled a coffee mill, then cranked into the firing chamber.

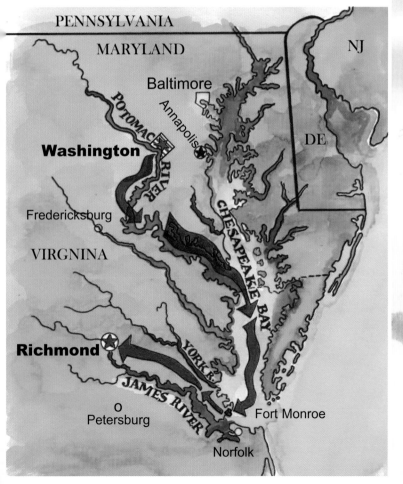

PENNSYLVANIA

MARYLAND

NJ

Baltimore

Annapolis

DE

Washington

POTOMAC RIVER

Fredericksburg

VIRGNINA

CHESAPEAKE BAY

Richmond

YORK R.

JAMES RIVER

O
Petersburg

Fort Monroe

Norfolk

Designed by William Ager, the weapon was first used at Lee's Mill during the Warwick-Yorktown siege on April 16.

15

The Confederates countered with the rapid-fire gun designed by Captain R. S. Williams of the 4th Kentucky Cavalry. It fired a one-pound projectile as far as 2,000 yards at a rate of 65 rounds per minute. The gun required a three-man crew to operate it.

The **Williams Rapid Fire Gun** went into action at Blue Springs, Tennessee, in October 1863. Today one of these weapons is on display at the West Point Museum; another at the Virginia Military Institute.

The **Gatling Gun** came along late in the war but its use was very limited.

Firing All 25 Cylinders

The **first practical rapid-fire gun** to be used in the
Civil War was invented in 1861 by **Dr. Josephus Requa**
(standing at left), a **dentist** from Rochester, New York.
In his younger days, Requa had worked as a gunsmith.
He made a sketch of his concept, then consulted with
his old gunsmith mentor, William Billinghurst at his
shop on Main Street. Billinghurst liked the idea and
made the first working model.

The weapon had 25 barrels, each 24 inches long.
A long clip held 25 bullets which lined up with
each barrel. The first model cost $500 to make
and weighed about 700 pounds.

Here's how it worked.
The hammer was manually cocked, then released
by pulling the lanyard, causing the hammer to
strike a percussion cap that fired all the bullets
simultaneously.

17

Requa went to Washington in April 1861 and tried to sell his weapon to the Chief of Ordnance Procurement, Brigadier General James W. Ripley, who was stubbornly resistant to change.

It's a good gun, but a platoon of soldiers could fire just as rapidly.

Undaunted Requa got a local dentist, Dr. Edward Maynard, to give him a letter of introduction to President Lincoln. At their meeting Lincoln was so impressed by Requa's concept that he ordered General Ripley to arrange a demonstration at the Washington Navy Yard.

On the day of the demonstration, there was a man next to Requa with a new breech-loading cannon. However, during his test, a shell got jammed in the tube. So for safety's sake the president left before Requa successfully fired his weapon.

KRUMPH!

The Requa Rapid-Fire Gun

was never officially adopted by the military since no final report was ever issued by the Ordnance section of the War Department. The gun did perform so well during its many tests that a number of regiments ordered and deployed this new gun in the Petersburg campaign and the battle of Cold Harbor.

The Navy also used two of them on Admiral Porter's Western Flotilla.

Used mainly as a defensive weapon, Requa guns guarded the Union flanks at their siege of Fort Wagner, South Carolina, in July 1863.

Today, Requa guns are on display at the Springfield Armory National Historic Site in Springfield, Massachusetts, the museum at West Point, New York, the Kentucky Military Museum in Frankfort, Kentucky, and the Smithsonian Insitution in Washington.

Land mines

were first used when the Confederates retreated from their Warwick-Yorktown Line on April 30, 1862. General Gabriel Rains ordered his troops to bury 8 and 10-pound artillery shells a few inches below ground.

These "torpedoes" only slightly delayed the Federal advance into Yorktown. Later Confederate prisoners were used to dig up the "infernal machines."

They were primed with fulminate (a detonating acid) or with an ordinary artillery friction primer and set to explode when stepped on or moved.

Hand Grenades

were used by both sides during the war. Most were 2.4 inches in diameter, 4½ inches long, and weighed three pounds. Others were 2.9 inches thick, 6½ inches long, and weighed 5 pounds.

The weapon had paper fins to guide it so it would land on its plunger.

On impact the plunger would sink into the bomb... causing a spark that would ignite the explosive.

If the grenade did not land precisely on its plunger, it failed to go off.

WHAP

The enemy soldier simply picked it up and threw it back.

WINANS' STEAM GUN

Ross Winans, a wealthy Southern sympathizer, built a *steam gun* in his locomotive factory in Baltimore, Maryland, in the spring of 1861.

The city of Baltimore purchased the weapon for $2,500 on behalf of the Confederacy and shipped it by rail to Harpers Ferry.

However, the 6th Massachusetts Regiment stopped the train at Ellicott's Mills and took the gun to the town of Relay, Maryland.

The Yankees could not get the gun to fire because Mr. Winans did not ship all of the parts.

Soon afterwards Winans was arrested as a secessionist and imprisoned at Fort McHenry in Baltimore. He was released later that summer.

Does the armor suit you?

At the start of the Civil War some businessmen in such cities as Boston, Philadelphia, and New York ironed out a scheme to make money by tailoring bullet-proof vests for the wealthier volunteers.

The vests were so popular that sutlers (peddlers who followed the troops) carried them.

An armored vest consisted of shaped iron plates about one-sixteenth of an inch thick. Soldiers used them at the battles of Shiloh and Antietam.

A vest could deflect a musket ball.

However, against rifled bullets they were useless.

With all the equipment, rations, and ammunition that a soldier carried, these heavy vests were an added, uncomfortable burden. Many infantrymen tossed them aside on long marches in the hot sun.

Prof. T.S.C. Lowe

The Gigantic Gas Bag

On June 17, 1861, a giant balloon called the *Enterprise* was inflated with 20,000 cubic feet of hydrogen, then rose 500 feet above Washington, DC, trailing a telegraph wire.

Professor Thaddeus Sobieski Constantine Lowe piloted the aircraft in an effort to prove its value to the military. He tapped out a telegram to President Lincoln.

Sir, this point of observation commands an area nearly 50 miles in diameter.

This telegram is now in the Air and Space Museum.*

Later the crew towed the balloon through the streets and anchored it on the White House lawn. The next day President Lincoln came out to take a closer look at it.

*Special Footnote—Professor Lowe lifted off and landed his balloon at the Washington Armory which was torn down in 1964 to make room for the Air & Space Museum.

The Confederate Rocket Forces

The general was impressed so he scheduled another test which he centered around a gala picnic with an extensive list of officers, wives, and local politicians. Kellersberger knew the rocket needed a lot of work, so when the big day arrived he conveniently came down with a headache and could not attend.

So, an inexperienced lieutenant took charge of the test. One rocket exploded on its launch pad. The next one went out of control and tore into the grandstand at which point all hell broke loose.

Swiss-born Getulius Kellersberger was chief engineer for the Confederate army in Texas and as such was project officer for a rocket battery in San Antonio. In his command was a German mechanic who claimed to have built rockets in the Austria-Hungarian War. He convinced Kellersberger to let him build the rockets for the Confederates.

The first test was mildly successful.

That night the general scrubbed the Confederate rocket program.

Christmas 1862 in Virginia started out as a depressing day for **Hood's Texas Brigade** until Captain James "Old Tarantula" Reilly challenged the men to

A TEXAS-SIZE SNOWBALL BATTLE.

With flags flying, drums beating, and horns blaring, the Texans sallied forth, their cartridge pouches filled with snowballs, and they attacked everything in sight.

Even the oldest officers forgot their years and dignity to become boys again, as **10,000** fought the Civil War's most civil battle.

27

A Confederate Drug Lab

Samuel Preston Moore of **South Carolina**, Surgeon General of the Confederacy, anticipated the shortage of drugs in the South caused by the Union blockade. So he set up medical laboratories to manufacture medicines at Lincolnton and Charlotte, North Carolina; Columbia, South Carolina; Mobile and Montgomery, Alabama; and Macon and Atlanta, Georgia.

The **only** lab west of the Mississippi River was located about six miles east of **Tyler, Texas** at a place known as

Headache Springs.

The site was chosen because the mineral waters of the spring were known to heal aches, pains, and "whatever else ails you."

Under the direction of a Doctor Johnson from Virginia, technicians mixed the waters of Headache Springs with local herbs—poke root, snakeroot, Jerusalem oak, Jimson weed, nightshade, cherry bark, and mistletoe—to produce medicines and whiskey for the Confederacy.

The Confederate "Alcatraz"

Alcatraz is an island in San Francisco Bay, California, first used as a military prison in 1909. It served as a federal penitentiary from 1934 to 1963 and was considered escape-proof. This is the story of an earlier, escape-proof federal prison that stood on an island.

To protect New York from an attack by the British during the War of 1812, the U.S. government constructed a fort on Hendrick's Reef in the Narrows about 200 yards from the Brooklyn shore. Originally called Fort Diamond because of its shape. it was renamed in 1825 after a Revolutionary War general who was visiting New York...

Fort Lafayette.

Through the years, due to changing tides and the expansion of Brooklyn's land mass into the Narrows, the distance from the island to the mainland shrank to a hundred yards.

After a quarter century of wear and tear, the fort was woefully outdated. It needed so many repairs that the government decided to virtually rebuild it. During part of its reconstruction in 1841 the officer in charge was a 34 year-old captain of the Army Engineers by the name of **Robert E. Lee**.

Fort Lafayette became the first prisoner-of-war facility in the northern states on July 15, 1861, when Edward D. Townsed, assistant adjutant general of the Army, ordered Major General Nathaniel P. Banks to house POWs there. The first POWs arrived on July 22.

Along with captured soldiers, the prison held Southern sympathizers including members of the Maryland legislature and the police commissioners of the city of Baltimore.

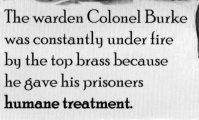

The warden Colonel Burke was constantly under fire by the top brass because he gave his prisoners **humane treatment.**

Burke's biggest problem was his guards taking bribes to look the other way during an escape.

One inmate made a life jacket out of cans and...

kerchiefs which he purchased from none other than the warden. Unfortunately he drowned when the contraption came apart in the water.

The last prisoner was released a year after the war ended, making this facility the **last** major Union prison to hold a POW.

The fort was almost destroyed by a fire on December 1, 1868.

The U.S. Navy stored ammunition in the fort during both world wars. For a while there was talk of making it into a **nightclub**.

Fort Lafayette was demolished in the early 1960s to become a caisson to hold up the east tower of the **Verrazano~Narrows Bridge**.

The U.S. Capitol was among the buildings in Washington torched by the British during the War of 1812. Congress quickly appropriated funds to erect this building in 1815 at First and A Streets.

The lawmakers met here until 1829. When Congress moved back to its permanent location, this building became known as **the old brick capitol.**

By the outbreak of the Civil War the old capitol was an abandoned, dilapidated mess.

It will make an ideal prison for Confederate officers, spies, blockade runners, and smugglers.

The most famous inmates of the old Capitol Prison were female Confederate spies.

An early tenant was **Rose O'Neal Greenhow** who tipped off Rebel General Pierre Beauregard on the Union's strategy at Bull Run. Even in prison she managed to smuggle gle messages to her contacts.

Belle Boyd helped Stonewall Jackson win the Shenandoah Valley Campaign of 1862. Her boyfriend, C. W. D. Smitley, a West Virginia cavalryman, turned her in to the Old Capitol Prison. She taunted her guards with insults and constantly singing Confederate songs.

Lookee here, a baboon wearing a blue suit!

The Old Capitol Prison was torn down in 1932.

Major General Benjamin Franklin **Butler** was commander of the Department of the Gulf in 1862. The women of New Orleans were giving his troops a hard time, which prompted Butler to issue his infamous **Order Number 28**.

Oops! I thought y'all were **pigs**.

Go back home, you blue-bellied devil.

Any female who insults or shows contempt for any soldier of the United States shall be regarded as a woman of the town plying her vocation.

The edict outraged northerners and southerners alike. People called Butler

THE BEAST.

The insults stopped, but reports of financial hanky-panky forced Butler's removal in December 1862. He spent the rest of the war in command positions in Virginia and North Carolina. After he failed to take Fort Fisher, North Carolina, General U.S. Grant relieved him from any future commands.

Long after the war ended **chamber pots** with Butler's portrait were found in many southern homes.

Captain Sally

Sally Louisa Tompkins was born on November 9, 1833, on the Poplar Grove Plantation in Matthews County, Virginia. After her father's death, and with a considerable inheritance, Sally moved with her mother to Richmond.

In June 1861 the Confederate government appealed to the public to help care for soldiers wounded at the Battle of Bull Run.

At the time Sally was 27 years old and unmarried. She persuaded her neighbor, Judge John Robertson to donate his mansion at 3rd and Main Streets for use as a **hospital.**

Sally took her mother's cook and opened the hospital on July 1st. Although Sally had no training as a nurse, her patients recovered at an astounding rate.

36

A few months later President Jeff Davis signed an executive order that turned over all the private hospitals to the military. This meant that Miss Tompkins would be dismissed.

Not wanting to lose her valuable services, President Davis came up with a way to circumvent his own regulation...

I am granting you a commission as a **captain** in the Confederate cavalry.

She turned down a salary but pulled rank to obtain medicine, equipment, and other medical supplies.

Until it closed on June 13, 1865, **1,333 patients** were treated at Captain Sally's hospital.

Only 73 died there.

Captain Sally became a popular celebrity in postwar Virginia. She died in 1916 at the age of eighty-three in the Confederate Women's Home in Richmond and was given a full military funeral because she was **the only woman officer in the Confederate army.** Four chapters of the United Daughters of the Confederacy are named in her honor.

The Nuns of the Battlefield

Prior to 1860 Catholic nuns had established 28 hospitals in the United States.

When the Civil War started in 1861 nuns were the only group of women experienced in both nursing and hospital management.

Of all the nurses on the battlefield, about 600 were nuns from over a dozen orders. Many were born in Ireland or of Irish descent.

One of the most famous was Eliza Maria Gillespie, known as **Mother Angela**, originally from Brownsville, Pennsylvania. Her parents hailed from County Donegal, Ireland.

Gillespie had become a nun in 1853 and took the name **Sister Mary of St. Angela**. Within a few years she was the Mother Superior of St. Mary's Academy, now **St. Mary's College** at **Notre Dame**, Indiana.

During the war Mother Angela's Sisters of the Holy Cross nursed both Confederate and Union casualties.

Early in the war wounded soldiers were transported to hospitals in cattle cars. As time went on these rail cars were equipped with kitchens, beds, and actual surgeries. This was the forerunner of M.A.S.H.– Mobile Army Surgical Hospital.
The **Sisters of Charity** worked on these mobile hospitals.

Among the Sisters of Charity were 38 from Ireland including Sister Mary O'Donnell.

These sisters are honored by **The Nuns of the Battlefield Memorial** in Washington, DC. When it was dedicated in 1924 by the Ancient Order of Hibernians Ladies Auxiliary, Sister Mary O'Donnell of the Sisters of Mercy was the only Civil War nun at the ceremony.

Feminist in Trousers

Mary Edwards Walker was born in 1832 in Oswego, New York. At 16 she was teaching school in New York City. To promote her campaign for **women's rights** she started to wear **trousers** which caused a scandal in Victorian society.

Consequently, most women snubbed her and kids pelted her with rotten eggs.

The professions were closed to women, but that did not stop Mary from earning a **doctorate in medicine** from **Syracuse University** in 1855. She married another physician, Albert Miller in 1856 and kept her own name. They started a medical practice in Rome, NY but the public was not ready for a female doctor so their business went under. They split up 3 years later.

At the outbreak of the Civil War Dr. Walker tried to join the army but was denied a commission as a medical officer. She volunteered anyway and served as an assistant surgeon—**the first woman surgeon in the U.S. Army.** As an unpaid doctor she was assigned to the hospital in the U.S. Patent Office in Washington.

For the next two years she worked as a field surgeon, caring for casualties from the battles of Fredericksburg, Chattanooga, and Chickamauga.

Finally, in September 1863 Major General George Thomas appointed Mary assistant surgeon with the rank of major in the **52nd Ohio Infantry** based in Chattanooga, Tennessee. She donned a slightly modified version of a Union officer's uniform and sported two pistols at all times. Major Walker often ventured away from the unit and crossed Confederate lines to care for injured civilians.

Her ability to travel freely between enemy and friendly lines prompted rumors on both sides that she was really a **spy**.

On one of these forays, Mary was taken prisoner by the Rebels on April 10, 1864, and confined in Castle Thunder in Richmond for a period of four months.

In her later years, Mary enjoyed telling how she was released in a "man for man" exchange for a Confederate major. She returned to her medical work in Kentucky and Tennessee but was never allowed to go near the front lines.

Major Generals William T. Sherman and George H. Thomas recommended the Medal of Honor be awarded to Major Mary Walker for her meritorious service to the wounded. Congress approved it and President Andrew Johnson bestowed it on her on November 11, 1865.

Major Mary Edwards Walker is the only woman in American history to receive the Medal of Honor, the country's highest military decoration.

After the war Mary became a writer and toured the lecture circuit on behalf of the "Bloomer Girls," speaking out on behalf of women's rights, temperance, health, and the right for women to wear trousers. She took pride in the many times she was arrested for "masquerading as a man."

Mary used her court appearances to expound the philosophy of the "Bloomer Girls," a group of women who advocated women's rights and the wearing of trousers.

Corsets and hoop skirts are not only **unhealthy**, they are lascivious fashions invented by the prostitutes of Paris.

Each time the judge acquitted Mary when she read a special act of Congress that gave her permission to wear men's clothing because of her war record.

Mary's tactics caused her to break away from the "Bloomer Girls" which meant the loss of income from her lectures.

She was later fired from a job in the Patent Office for insubordination.

43

In 1917 the government ruled that the Medal of Honor be given only for "actual combat with the enemy." Consequently, the government revoked the medals of over 900 recipients including Mary Walker who was living on a $20 a month military pension. When the Army asked Mary to return her medal...

the 85 year-old veteran replied...

Over my dead body!

Mary went to Washington to argue her case before Congress. It was an exercise in futility. On her way out she fell down the Capitol steps. Her health deteriorated. She died two years later in Oswego, New York and was buried with her Medal of Honor.

President Jimmy Carter restored her medal in 1977. The U.S. Postal Service issued this commemorative stamp in 1982 for the sesquicentennial of Dr. Walker's birth.

By the way—Mary Walker affects our lives today. She came up with the idea of using a return postcard for registered mail.

Dr. Mary Walker
Army Surgeon

Medal of Honor
USA 20c

THE TREASURY GIRLS

Military service depleted the country's manpower between 1861 and 1865.

Therefore the U.S. government hired women to work in such places as the arsenal, navy yard, and government printing office in Washington.

About 600 "Treasury girls" worked mainly in the currency section cutting apart sheets of paper money. Their pay of $50 a month was hardly enough to live on in the capital's inflated economy.

After the war ended most female govern~ment employees were let go or replaced by men.

The Queen of the Confederacy

Lucy Holcombe was born June 11, 1832, in **Tennessee**. Around 1848 her family moved to Marshall, Texas. When she was 19 her fiance was killed on an ill-fated expedition to liberate Cuba. From then on, she lived her life in the fast lane, hob-nobbing with men of power, wealth, and influence.

On a trip to the ritzy Virginia seashore she met **Francis W. Pickens**, 48, a widower, plantation owner, and politician from South Carolina.

Pickens was smitten with Lucy and wrote long love letters to her in Texas, begging her to marry him. Realizing she had a live one on the hook, Lucy promised her hand in marriage, but only if Francis could land an ambassadorship in some exotic locale.

Jumping at the chance to wed Lucy, Pickens used all of his political clout to wrangle an appointment as ambassador to Russia from President James Buchanan. They were married in Marshall, Texas, on April 29, 1858, then sailed to Russia. Lucy's intelligence and friendliness made her a big hit in the court of Czar Alexander.

When Pickens' term ended in 1860, he and Lucy returned to his home in South Carolina. Pickens was asked to run for governor of the Palmetto State. He did and won. On December 24, 1860, he seceded his state from the Union, the first governor to do so.

When her daughter was born, the Czar and Czarina became the child's godparents.

The following April the first shots of the Civil War were fired in South Carolina when Fort Sumter was hit by shore batteries in Charleston Harbor.

Lucy wielded a lot of influence on the affairs of state because her husband, South Carolina Governor Francis Pickens, relied heavily on her advice. She unraveled many knotty problems and helped finance the war effort by hocking her silver and jewels, thus earning her the sobriquet,

Queen of the Confederacy.

She designed the flag of the Holcombe Legion of South Carolina, named in her honor, embellishing it with the star of Texas.

Her picture was placed on Confederate money, one on the one-dollar note issued June 2, 1862, the other on the $100 bill issued December 2, 1862. She is the only southern woman to achieve that distinction.

Lucy died on August 8, 1899, and is buried next to her husband and daughter in Edgefield County Cemetery.

THE LOST GOLD MYSTERY

In the spring of 1863 some bankers in Wheeling, West Virginia, loaded some boxes on a wagon then covered them with hay.

Earlier that day they had stashed twenty-six bars of solid gold, each weighing fifty pounds into a false bottom of that wagon.

Then, one of the bank executives handed a sealed envelope to a young Army lieutenant.

The envelope contained special orders for his eyes only.

You are to deliver a secret cache of gold to Washington. Avoid contact with the enemy. Nobody is to know the contents of the wagon.

His orders were to proceed as far
north as necessary to avoid any possibility
of running into Rebel patrols, then turn south and
head for Washington. Accompanying the lieutenant were
eight cavalrymen and a civilian guide by the name of Connors.

There was something else the expedition had to
avoid—Copperheads—an underground organization of
southern sympathizers living in the northern states.

The lieutenant's plan was to trek north to the town of Driftwood in the heart of Pennsylvania's lumber country, build a raft, and float down the Susquehanna River to Harrisburg, then drive overland to Washington.

Throughout the journey the lieutenant suffered from one fever after another and had to ride in the wagon. While he was laid up, the civilian guide took charge of the mission.

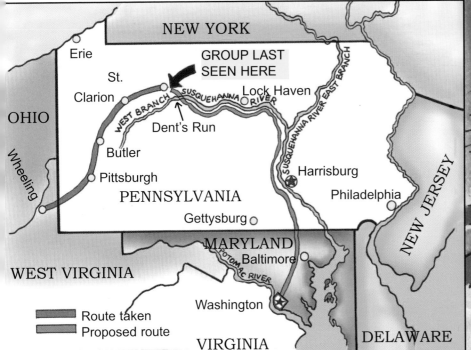

They camped near the town of St. Marys on the last Saturday in June. That night the young officer got so delirious that he blurted out the secret of the gold cargo which came as a shocking surprise to the escorting soldiers.

On Sunday morning the gold-laden expedition broke camp and turned southeast toward the town of Driftwood.

Connors was still in command as the group rode into what is now Pine Tree Trail State Forest.

They were never seen again.

Fifty miles east of St. Marys lies the town of Lock Haven, Pennsylvania where, two months later...

One day in September 1863 a disheveled, mumbling Connors, the guide for the gold shipment, staggered into Lock Haven,

....ambush...
...murder....
...all gone....

Immediately the Army sent investigators to "grill" Connors who claimed the expedition was ambushed by bandits who killed all the soldiers, stole the gold, and left him for dead. The Army did not buy his story.

53

So the Army hired Pinkerton detectives to search the area but all they found were some dead mules near the village of Dent's Run, just off the West Branch of the Susquehanna River about ten miles west of the town of Driftwood.

Connors was drafted into the Army and sent to a remote fort out west. The Army refused ever to discharge him.

He became an alcoholic and often said he knew where the gold was hidden, but when he was sober he could not remember anything.

In the early 1870s some human skeletons, believed to be those of the soldiers were found in the same area.

Allegedly, the federal government searched the area around Dent's Run as late as the 1940s but none of the gold was ever found. Some believe it is still hidden in the Allegheny Mountains of Pennsylvania.

The Maryland Gold Mine

The story of the Maryland gold mine started with **Senator Edward D. Baker** of Oregon, a founder of the Republican Party and good friend of President Lincoln. He got the idea of organizing one of the many "theme regiments" popular at the beginning of the war. **Colonel Baker's California Regiment** would consist of men who at one time or another lived in California and Oregon.

Pennsylvania, not California, adopted Baker's scheme and he organized four California regiments. They became known as the Philadelphia Brigade, the only brigade in either army to be named after a city. When Pennsylvania came up short on its recruiting goals, the state absorbed the brigade and named it the **71st Pennsylvania**.

One day in 1861 after the Battle of Bull Run the 71st Pennsylvania was encamped near **Great Falls** on the Potomac River in Montgomery County, **Maryland.**

One of Colonel Baker's men was a Private McCleary, a Californian who was so smitten by gold fever that wherever his regiment camped...

McCleary panned for gold, including the the streams around Great Falls.

Lo and behold, he hit pay dirt, enough to start a gold mine in Maryland.

Private McCleary never said a word about his discovery of gold at Great Falls, Maryland. More important, he managed to survive the war.

McCleary returned to Maryland after the war and purchased the land on which he made his discovery, near the town of Cropley, now part of the C&O Canal National Historic Park.

He started the Maryland Gold Mine Company in 1867 and sank a shaft 100 feet from atop a hill. Between 1868 and 1869 he sifted out about eleven ounces of gold worth **$20.69** an ounce. A few years later he sold the mine.

Over the years various companies operated and enlarged McCleary's mine. More than 5,000 ounces of gold worth over **$150,000** had come out of this and other small mines around Great Falls by the time mining ceased in the 1950s.

Confederate Postage Stamps

Created on February 21, 1861, the **Confederate Post Office** Department was the only government of either side to make a **profit** during the war. Running the show was Postmaster General **John Henninger Reagan** of Texas.

The first thing he did was entice pro southern executives at the Postal Department in Washington to join his staff.

They arrived in Richmond with reports, maps, and files which they "appropriated" from their old jobs.

This material will help us build our own postal system.

The U.S. Postal Service continued to deliver mail to the seceded states even after the war broke out. That stopped on June 1st when...

Reagan placed 8,535 post offices in the south under his control.

...and we will no longer use U.S. postage stamps.

Prior to this there had been a total of 28,586 post offices in the U.S.

Reagan also stipulated,

> ...until our stamps are printed, postmasters will accept cash and stamp "paid" on the envelope.

Some postmasters designed special stick-ons for their towns and had them produced in local printing shops.
They are known to collectors as

postmaster provisionals

because...they were used *provisionally* until Rebel stamps were issued.

Unable to use state-of-the-art printers in northern cities, Postmaster General Reagan commissioned lithographers **Hoyer and Ludwig** of Richmond, Virginia, to design and print stamps for the Confederacy. Hoyer and Ludwig could not obtain metal plates so they printed on heavy stones. The stamps were usually printed in one or two colors; black was considered a color.

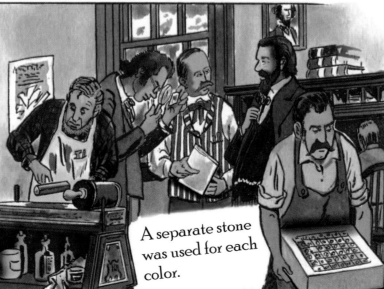

A separate stone was used for each color.

Charles Ludwig designed the first Confederate stamps and drew them freehand.

59

Issued on October 16, 1861, the five cent Jefferson Davis was the **first** American stamp to depict a **living president.**

Rebel stamps were not perforated and had to be cut apart with scissors.

Confederate stamps depicted southern heroes such as this ten-cent Chief Justice **John Marshall** designed by Mr. Ludwig.

Reagan was not happy with the quality of Hoyer and Ludwig's work so he ordered stamps from **Thomas de la Rue and Company** in London, England.

La Rue shipped five million stamps on the blockade runner *Bermuda*, but she was captured and her skipper threw all but a small package of stamps overboard.

The next year Rebel stamps were being printed in Richmond, this time by Archer and Daly Lithographers.

Frederick Halpern of Archer and Daly designed this two-cent Andrew Jackson.

When General Grant and his armies closed in on Richmond, the plates were sent to Columbia, **South Carolina,** where **Keating and Bull** produced stamps until General Sherman raided that city.

In all, the South commissioned seventeen stamps. Only one, the **John C. Calhoun** one, was delivered, stored, but never used.

After the war ended in 1865 a Union soldier found the John C. Calhoun stamps and made an envelope out of one of the sheets.

On the back of another sheet he wrote a letter home.

Over the years the letter and the envelope were sold to separate collectors.

As the war dragged on, paper became scarce in the South. People wrote letters on wallpaper, music sheets, and anything that resembled paper.

Letters that went overseas had a two-cent surcharge for the captain of the blockade runner.

After Vicksburg fell on July 4, 1863, the federals controlled the Mississippi. Southerners who sent letters to places in the west paid extra postage for smugglers to take the mail across the river in half-sunken boats at night.

When the war ended, the U.S. Post Office Department was faced with the enormous task of kick-starting mail delivery in the southern states.

The job went slowly. By December 1865 some 500 mail routes had been restored. But a year later only 3,234 of the 8,902 prewar post offices in the South were up and running in the federal system.

A few weeks after the war ended Confederate Postmaster General John Reagan was traveling with President Jefferson Davis and Texas Governor Francis Lubbock when they were captured near **Abbeville, Georgia.**

Reagan died 22 weeks in solitary confinement at Fort Warren in Boston Harbor.
On his release he went home to Texas and was elected to the United States House of Representatives in 1874.

As chairman of the U.S. House Committee on Commerce, in 1887 Reagan helped establish the **Interstate Commerce Commission.**

It's in the can

Other than weapons that came into common use during the Civil War, an everyday household item was popularized during that conflict—canned food. A British merchant Peter Durand, who came up with the "tin canister" in 1810, had a contract to supply preserved foods to the Royal Navy.

An English immigrant, William Underwood introduced canning in the United States in 1817 when he opened a factory in Boston. At first his company preserved salmon and lobsters in glass bottles. Later they used tin canisters. It was his bookkeepers who first used the term "can."

Cans were opened with a hammer and chisel until....

Ezra J. Warner of Waterbury, Connecticut invented the **can opener** in 1858.

Having devised their own methods of opening cans, American families ignored Warner's opener, which was saved from oblivion when the Union military adopted it. The war created a critical need for canned rations, especially beans, green beans, oysters, and condensed milk.

64

In 1862 the U.S. War Department allowed the state of Iowa to form the 37th Iowa Infantry Regiment of **men over 45 years of age.** The average age ended up as 57. This 914-man unit was assembled that December at Camp Strong near Muscatine, Iowa.

The 37th Infantry became known as the

Iowa Graybeard Regiment.

Their drummer was Nicholas Ramey, age 72.

The oldest man was eighty year-old Private Curtis King. Six men were older than seventy; nearly all the members were over forty-five.

Colonel George Washington Kincaid commanded the regiment.

The Iowa Graybeards hiked and slept in the mud and rain like other soldiers but were exempt from combat jobs. Instead, they pulled guard duty in military prisons, rail yards, and arsenals in Missouri, Tennessee, Indiana, Illinois and Ohio.

Only three were killed by enemy fire, but 145 died of disease, and 364 were discharged for medical reasons.

THE MONEY REGIMENT

When the war started New York City's militia units all left for Washington. Concerns over the city's security led some **insurance** and **banking firms** to put up the money to field six infantry regiments. On May 13, 1861, they organized the **22nd Regiment,** which became part of the New York State Militia on September 17, 1861.

It soon numbered some 400 well-to-do gentlemen who **purchased their own** specially designed **uniforms**. Their dashing gray uniforms with touches of red earned them the nickname, **Strawberry Grays.** Later, since their gray frock coats looked like those of the Confederates, they exchanged them for blue fatigue jackets.

The state of New York was short on funds, so the 22nd Regiment purchased their own weapons: Enfield rifles and sword bayonets from England. They saw action at Harper's Ferry, Gettysburg, and were called home to the New York City Draft Riots of 1863.

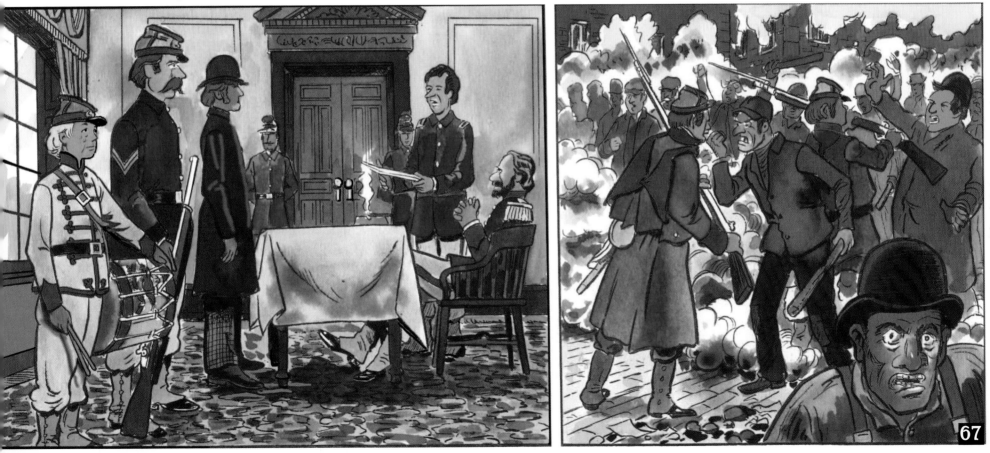

67

A Most Unusual Army Mascot

A group of Ojibwa Indians killed an eagle in Chippewa County, Wisconsin, around the early spring of 1861.

Chief Sky climbed to the aerie and captured two of the mother eagle's offspring, then took them to the town of Jim Falls.

There he traded one of the eaglets to Mrs. Margaret McCann for a bushel of corn.

Several months later, Mrs. McCann's husband Don sold the young eagle to Lieutenant James McGuire, a member of Company C, 8th Regiment of the Wisconsin Volunteer Infantry, known as the "Eau Claire Badgers." With the eagle on a tether, the regiment marched to Madison to train at Fort Randall.

The company commander, Captain John E. Perkins named the eagle "Old Abe" in honor of the commander-in-chief.

Designated the official mascot of the 8th Wisconsin, Old Abe accompanied the Badgers to Mississippi. He always stayed with Company C and was carried on a perch held by one of his handlers David McLain.

The 8th Wisconsin changed its nickname from the Badgers to the Eagle Regiment. With Old Abe on his perch mounted atop a shield, the regiment fought in over 35 battles including Vicksburg and Corinth, Mississippi.

In one account, Old Abe flew high over the battlefield adding his screams to the din of battle. Despite being shot through the wing at Corinth, Old Abe survived.

After the war Old Abe appeared at veterans reunions and patriotic events across the country. Back in Madison, the eagle had special quarters in the basement of the Wisconsin State Capitol but he died from a fire near his room. He was stuffed and put on a perch in the State Assembly Room until a fire destroyed his body in 1904.

During World War I the 101st Division was created in November 1918 but was demobilized a short time later when the war ended. It was reconstituted as the 101st Division of the Organized Reserves in Milwaukee, Wisconsin, in 1921. Someone designed a shoulder patch with Old Abe on his old shield. The War Department OK'd the present version in 1923.

The "Airborne" tab was added in 1942 when the 101st Reserves was replaced by the 101st Airborne Division with Old Abe still on their shoulder patch. The "Screaming Eagles" have proudly served in every American conflict from D-Day in World War II to Vietnam to Iraqi Freedom.

AIRBORNE

Fort Myer, Virginia, was named after Albert James Myer of Buffalo, New York. While serving as assistant surgeon at **Fort Davis, Texas,** in 1855 Myer was inspired by the signals used by the Comanches and Apaches.

MYER DEVELOPED A SYSTEM OF SIGNALING USING
TORCHES AND WIG-WAG FLAGS
WHICH THE U.S. ARMY OFFICIALLY ADOPTED IN 1859.

Drawings based on Myers' Manual of Signals, 1864.

Myer was promoted to major in 1861 and put in charge of the newly formed Army **Signal Corps** headquartered at Fort Whipple, VA, now Fort Myer.

The Recipe for Roasting the Big Apple

In October 1864 Lt. Colonel Robert Martin and seven Southern agents calling themselves **the Confederate Army of Manhattan** left Canada, traveled south, and secretly entered New York City.

They planned to lead 20,000 Sons of Liberty (southern loyalists) on a rampage of terror on Election Day, November 8, 1864.

Policemen who were clandestine members of the Sons of Liberty would seize police headquarters and other government buildings.

By nightfall the city would **secede** from the Union and become **the Free Port of New York.**

Simultaneously an uprising would be launched by the Sons of Liberty in **Chicago.**

Two days before Election Day federal agents and Confederate informers broke the conspiracy. Colonels Grenfell and Marmaduke, the ringleaders in Chicago, were captured.

Immediately 10,000 Union troops marched into New York and took up strategic positions around the city.

The Confederate Army of Manhattan decided to postpone their day of terror to November 25.

Eight southern agents calling themselves the Confederate Army of Manhattan decided to set fire to the city when their plans for a riot fizzled.

On November 25, 1864, Lt. John Headley, a Kentucky cavalryman, picked up a satchel from a chemist.

The satchel contained dozens of four-ounce bottles of **greek fire,** a clear liquid that bursts into flame as soon as it makes contact with air.

At their secret meeting place, Headley gave ten bottles each to five of his cohorts. Two Confederates failed to show up.

Each man had booked rooms under phony names in three or four hotels where they planned to start the fires.

At 8 p.m. Headley opened the gas jet in his room in the **Astor House** and poured the greek fire on his bed.

Headley left immediately to do the same to the City Hotel, Everett House, and the United States Hotel.

Simultaneously Lt. Colonel Robert Martin set fire to his room in the Hoffman House, then did the same to the Fifth Avenue and St. Denis Hotels.

Captain Robert Cobb Kennedy torched the Tammany, Lovejoy, and New England Hotels.

Lieutenant John Ashbrook started fires in the LaFarge and St. Nicholas Hotels.

Lieutenant James Chenault hit the Howard Hotel, then joined up with Kennedy and headed for P. T. Barnum's Museum.

Within quick succession alarms were sounding across the city, from the United States Hotel at Fulton Street to the Hudson River docks.

At 9:15 p.m. Chenault and Kennedy entered Barnum's Museum on Broadway, paid the thirty-cents admission, and went upstairs to the exhibits on the third floor. Barnum's was not on their agenda for destruction, the two terrorists just wanted to take a break there for a while. Kennedy, who had been drinking, pulled a bottle of Greek fire from his jacket and threw it at the wooden stairs. It smashed and the phosphorus burst into flame. When the foul-smelling fumes spread into the exhibit areas, people started running in a frenzy. The only injuries were some scrapes and bruises.

Fortunately for New Yorkers the Greek fire was not very strong, so the fires were extinguished before they did much damage.

The Confederate Army of Manhattan managed to slip out of the city. Colonel Martin, the leader, and Lt. Headley took a train to Canada. Later they collaborated on a book about the incident.

Only one of the Confederates paid for the fire caper with his life. Captured in Michigan Captain Kennedy was brought to Fort Lafayette in New York harbor and hanged on March 25, 1865.

By the way:
Lt. Ashbrook torched the LaFarge Hotel located next door to the Winter Garden Theater. Performing there that night with his two older brothers was **John Wilkes Booth.**

The Northernmost Engagement in the Civil War

The Confederate State Department opened a "consulate" at the St. Lawrence Hotel in Montreal, Canada, ostensibly to maintain diplomatic relations with Great Britain, but in reality, it was a base of operations for spies and saboteurs into the northern states of the Union.

Most of the southerners posted there were from rich plantations and their refined manner quickly endeared them to Montreal's high society.

Meanwhile, the Union decided to make it difficult for Confederate prisoners of war to escape to the South by establishing prison camps in the northernmost states. However, the Rebels who did manage to escape, merely fled to Canada.

In April 1864 Sergeant **Bennett Young** of Kentucky, a Confederate prisoner of war at Fort Douglas near Chicago, escaped into Canada, then made his way to Richmond.

There James A. Seddon, Secretary of War, promoted him to lieutenant in the Confederate *Special Services*.

Special Services consisted of about 67 officers and enlisted men. Seddon (standing) ordered these volunteers to return to Canada and carry out certain "enterprises," namely raids into towns along the United States' northern frontier.

Actually Bennett Young was the only one who would go on to make a significant contribution to the Rebel cause. On arriving in Montreal, he set out to recruit about 20 former prisoners of war for a special raiding party.

Besides Lt. Young, some *Special Servicemen* were: C. C. Clay the overall leader, George N. Saunders, Dr. Blackburn, Jacob Thompson, and **John Wilkes Booth**, seated on the right. No records exist of what Booth accomplished in Canada.

Young's orders and expense money were personally carried from Virginia by the renowned spy Sarah Slater, also known as Kate Thompson.

Lt. Young's mission was to take his men into the town of **St. Albans, Vermont,** and **rob all the banks.** Their escape back to Canada would be on horses stolen from the townspeople. The money would be delivered to Richmond for use by the Confederate government.

QUEBEC

Montreal

St. Albans

VERMONT

NEW YORK

Montpelier

NEW HAMPSHIRE

Albany

MASSACHUSETTS

Boston

80

St. Albans was a quiet village about fifteen miles south of the Canadian border. Lt. Young and two of his men arrived there on October 10, 1864.

Ticket Office

They checked into the Tremont House.

...you fellas from around here?

We come from St. Johns, Canada.

...on a sporting vacation.

Every day for the following week, three or four of Young's men arrived. Some got rooms in the Tremont House; others stayed at the American House. On the morning of October 19 all were present for duty and ready to go into action.

Lt. Young's raiders rushed through the village, pounding on doors, rounding up every citizen they could find, and herding them to the center of town. Then they threw off their overcoats revealing their Confederate uniforms. Lt. Young proclaimed,

This town is now in the hands of the Confederate States of America!

While some raiders stood guard in the streets, others fanned out and held up the village's three banks. As customers walked in they robbed them as well. Although they were professional soldiers, the were inept bank robbers. For example, while fumbling through a safe Marcus Spurr, Tom Collins, and Turner Treavis missed some $50,000 in U.S. bonds and a $50,000 block of ready-signed St. Albans Bank notes.

At the Franklin County Bank, Joe McCorty filled his pockets with cash, then emptied some coin bags only to find pennies, so he left them there, not knowing that one of the bags contained solid gold coins.

Nevertheless, this handful of amateurs robbed all the banks of St. Albans without firing a shot or injuring anyone, and hauled off some $208,000 for the Confederate States of America.

Lt. Young forced some bank officers and tellers to swear an oath of allegiance to the Confederacy and President Jefferson Davis.

Before leaving they tried to torch the town but only succeeded in burning down a wood shed.

To make their getaway the Rebels needed horses. Lt. Young and others "horse-jacked" theirs from riders on Main Street. Others pilfered Bedart's Saddle Shop of virtually its entire stock of saddles, bridles, and blankets. Then they rustled horses out of Fuller's Livery Stable. The owner, Ed Fuller showed up and asked...

What are you doing?

CLICK!

At the same time Lt. Young rode up and demanded Fuller hand over his spurs. Fuller pulled a derringer, pointed it at Young, and squeezed the trigger. It misfired and Fuller took off.

Lt. Young took aim at the fleeing livery stable owner. Fuller slipped behind a tree just as a carpenter named Elinus Morrison emerged from a nearby house and ran in front of Fuller. Young squeezed off a shot but Morrison caught the bullet in his stomach and died the following day. He was the only fatality of the raid.

With that, the Confederates raced out of St. Albans, heading for Canada.

Captain George P. Conyer, who had recently returned to St. Albans from the war, organized a posse and pursued the Confederates into Canada. At the international border the Vermonters met up with a detachment of Canadian militia who joined in the chase.

Over the next few weeks, they tracked down and captured thirteen raiders including Lt. Young. Most were taken by surprise in boarding houses then turned over to Canadian authorities. The rest of the raiders escaped for a while, but were caught in November.

The raiders were held in a Montreal jail, then went on trial in late November with Justice Charles J. Coursol presiding. Lt. Young gave his reasons for planning and executing the raid.

...obtain money for the cash-strapped Confederate treasury and stir up trouble on the Yankee frontier so that combat troops would be drawn away from the battle fronts in the South.

On December 13, Justice Coursol made his decision.

The courts of Canada have no jurisdiction in this matter. Therefore the defendants are free to go.

Meanwhile, during the trial, the U.S. government and the robbed banks of St. Albans demanded the prisoners be extradited to stand trial in the United States. Justice Smith who considered this request ruled that...

The transactions in St. Albans were acts of war. The Confederates are not liable for extradition.

Then there was the question of the **stolen money.** The Confederates absconded with $208,000, but **only $88,000 was recovered** when they were captured.

Whatever happened to the rest of the loot remains a **mystery.**

85

At the recommendation of Governor General Lord Monck (standing), the Provincial Parliament of Canada passed a bill to repay the three Vermont banks $50,000 (Canadian) in gold—then the equivalent of the $88,000 taken from the captured raiders. The money was then divided among the banks in proportion to their respective losses.

Lt. Young stayed in Canada until 1868. He returned home to Louisville, Kentucky, and became a lawyer and railroad executive. He got married and fathered a daughter. Later he was elected commander-in-chief of the United Confederate Veterans Association which carried the rank of Major General.

At the age of 68, in 1911, General Young informed the folks at St. Albans that he planned a vacation at the Ritz-Carlton in Montreal. The Vermonters sent a delegation of four men for a truly friendly visit. They toasted on Kentucky bourbon, and let bygones be bygones.

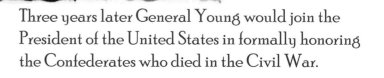

Three years later General Young would join the President of the United States in formally honoring the Confederates who died in the Civil War.

Congress formally buried the hatchet between the North and South in 1900 when it allowed Confederate soldiers buried in cemeteries around Washington, DC, to be reinterred in the Confederate section of Arlington National Cemetery.

On June 4, 1914, General **Bennett Young** joined **President Woodrow Wilson** and other dignitaries at the dedication ceremony of the **Confederate Monument** in the cemetery.

Halfway up the monument is a circular frieze of 32 life sized figures showing Southern soldiers going off to war.

Marching with the white Confederates is a **black soldier**, proving a fact that is overlooked or considered not politically correct to mention—African Americans served and fought in the Confederate army.

Photos by the artist-writer, with permission from Arlington National Cemetery

87

Blacks in Confederate Gray

Days after the first shots were fired at Fort Sumter, blacks throughout the South volunteered to enlist in the Confederate army and fight the enemies of their home turf. About a dozen free blacks from Salisbury, North Carolina, headed for the Atlantic coast to help stave off a possible amphibious landing by Yankee forces.

About 50,000 blacks served in the rebel army while some 300,000 African Americans, both slave and free, worked outside the military in support jobs such as rail yards, factories, sweat shops, hospitals, arsenals, and wharves.

Without the support of African Americans the South could not have carried on the war for four years.

On their own initiative free African Americans in the West started to organize companies of soldiers in such cities as Memphis and Nashville, Tennessee, and Fort Smith, Arkansas. The largest number of blacks enlisted in the Confederate militias hailed from Louisiana.

Most African Americans served as laborers building fortifications or as teamsters hauling weapons and supplies.

Also in the Confederate army were slaves who had accompanied their owners.

Abolitionist and former slave **Frederick Douglas** made this comment in the fall of 1861,

"There are many colored men in the Confederate army, not just as cooks and servants, but as real soldiers having muskets ready to shoot down loyal (Union) troops and do all...to destroy the American government and build up that of the rebels."

89

A *New York Times* correspondent reported seeing "A rebel artillery battery manned almost wholly by negroes, a single white man directing operations." In the West, African Americans fought with Confederate General Sterling Price's Frontier Army at the **Battle of Wilson's Creek, Missouri,** in early August 1861.

Meanwhile, **up north**, the war dragged on for over two years until the federal government organized the first official black regiments in May 1863.

This was not the case for the **United States Navy....**

NAVY BLUE AND BLACK

The U.S. Navy started to enlist **liberated slaves** in September 1861 and integrated them among white crews. By the end of the war nearly **30,000** African Americans, comprising **one-fourth of the Navy**, saw action on rivers, bayous, and the high seas.

Look Who's Listening

African American

During the war, Confederate President Jefferson Davis and his family lived in this house. ✱

One of Davis's slaves was his coachman, **William A. Jackson**. Unbeknownst to President Davis, Jackson was one of the most valuable **spies** for the Union.

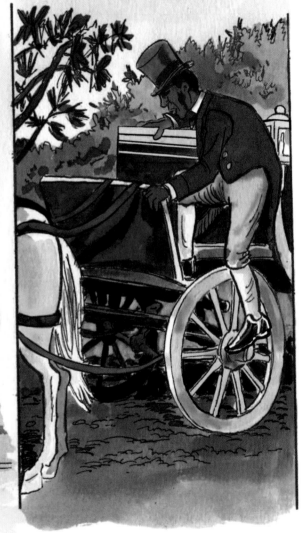

✱
Located at 12th and East Clay Streets, this is now part of the **Museum and White House of the Confederacy**, housing the largest collection of Confederate memorabilia in the world.

Jackson often overheard conversations that Davis had with his generals and members of his cabinet.

Later, he would steal away and pass the information to an accomplice. The accomplice relayed the information to another agent. The info moved along the intelligence pipeline until it landed in the hands of a G2 (Intel) officer at some Union military headquarters.

After the war William A. Jackson fell through the cracks of history and nothing is known about his later life.

Some of the best intelligence came from slaves working in southern homes and offices. **Mary Touvestre** was working for an engineer in southern Virginia in 1862.

We'll **raise** the sunken Union frigate **Merrimac** near Norfolk and cover her with **iron**.

A cast-iron beak will be bolted to her prow to **ram** Yankee ships and **smash** their **blockade**.

When her master was away Mary slipped into his office and **absconded** with a set of the plans.

94

She quickly fled north.

After a grueling trek she arrived in Washington and handed the plans to the U.S. Navy.

The Navy brass declared,

We must build an ironclad immediately!

Mary was questioned about the plans by **John Ericsson** who would design the Union's ironclad. Ericsson finalized his design and in a short time the U.S. Navy had its first ironclad "battleship," the **Monitor.**

Daniel Decatur Emmett was born in Mount Vernon, **Ohio**, in 1815. A self-taught musician, he joined a traveling circus, then organized the Virginia Minstrels in 1842. Along the way he composed *The Blue Tail Fly, Polly Wolly Doodle, Turkey in the Straw* and others. In 1859 he was writing songs for Bryant's Minstrels in New York City. One Saturday after the show closed Jerry Bryant asked him to write a "fast noisy song" by Monday.

That weekend the weather was wet and cold.

...reminds me of my days in the Virginia Minstrels.

On cold days in northern towns we used to say...

I wish I was in Dixie's land.

THAT'S IT!

On Monday morning Jerry Bryant had his new song.

...then I wish I was in Dixie's land. Hooray! Horray!

That Saturday, April 4, 1859, Bryant's Minstrels gave the **first performance** of *Dixie* in Mechanic's Hall at 472 Broadway.

Bryant's Minstrels went on the road and introduced **Dixie** to the country in their musical about the history of Jamestown, Virginia–*Pocohantas*. In February 1861 they were on stage in **Montgomery, Alabama**.

IN DIXIE'S LAND I'LL TAKE MY STAND TO LIVE AND DIE IN D

At the time Montgomery was the **capital** of the Confederacy. Bandsman Herman Arnold needed a song to play at the...

inauguration of **Jefferson Davis** as the **President** of the Confederate States of America.

A woman who had seen Bryant's show suggested,

Play *Dixie*. It has a pretty, catchy air.

So, on February 18, 1861, Arnold's band played *Dixie* as Jeff Davis rode in a parade from his hotel to the Capitol. Soon *Dixie* became the **unofficial anthem of the Confederacy.**

Bands in the north **refused** to play *Dixie*.

Composer Dan Emmett complained,

If I had known to what use they were to put my song, I never would have written it.

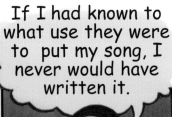

By the way—another writer, William Shakespeare Hays (1837–1907) claims to have written *Dixie*.

Emmett eventually sold all of his rights to *Dixie* to Firth, Pond, & Co. in New York City for **$300**.

Members of the Snowden Family of Knox County, Ohio, also contend that they composed the song.

On April 10, 1865, the day after Lee surrendered, President Lincoln gave a speech on the White House lawn.

Afterwards the President walked back to the Executive Mansion as the U.S. Marine Band played the song that Lincoln requested—*Dixie*.

Neither party could produce documented proof that they actually created *Dixie*. 97

On the morning of November 21, 1861, **Julia Ward Howe**, a young writer, suddenly awoke in the Willard Hotel in Washington. She was staying there with her husband Dr. Samuel Howe who was in town with the U.S. Sanitary Commission, forerunner of the Red Cross.

A poem is stirring in my mind and I must write it down before I forget it.

BATTLE HYMN

The previous afternoon Mrs. Howe was among some 75,000 people who watched a grand review of 70,000 Union soldiers on Munson Hill in the town of Bailey's Crossroads, Virginia. A special reviewing stand was built for President Lincoln, cabinet officers, the new commander of the Army General George McClellan, and foreign dignitaries.

Bailey's Crossroads was founded in 1837 by Hachaliah Bailey as a winter headquarters for his traveling circus. A descendant, George F. Bailey, sold the circus to P. T. Barnum in 1875 and the showman dubbed it **The Greatest Show on Earth.**

Mariah Bailey had her sons and some soldiers put up a circus tent and sold food to the spectators.

After the review thousands of civilians and soldiers went back to Washington over the Aqueduct Bridge, now the Key Bridge, the only bridge to the capital open to civilian traffic.

Julia Howe and her party were stuck in the worst traffic jam of the nineteenth century. The soldiers marching along were singing a popular song of the day.

Dr. James F. Clark, a Unitarian minister suggested to Julia...

Why don't you write some good words to go with that tune?

I wish I could do something for the war effort.

And so, the following morning Julia composed one of the most inspiring American songs, **The Battle Hymn of the Republic.**

Julia's **Battle Hymn** was published anonymously in the February 1862 issue of the *Atlantic Monthly*.

The magazine paid her **four dollars.**

THE STORY OF *TAPS*

Brigadier General Daniel **Butterfield**
of Utica, New York, was commanding
the 3rd Brigade of Morell's Division, 5th Corps at the battle of **Gaines' Mill**
near Richmond, Virginia, on June 26, 1862. His men began to fall back.

Despite being wounded Butterfield grabbed the colors
and rallied his troops. He was able to do this in the din
of battle because he had **composed several bugle calls**
to signal orders to his subordinate unit commanders.

100

This gained time for General George McClellan's Army of the Potomac to safely withdraw to **Harrison's Landing.**

For this action Butterfield was awarded the **Medal of Honor.**

At the Harrison's Landing campsite the army's morale was low. Men were suffering from mosquitoes, heat, typhoid, and dysentery.

Amid this misery, on July 2, 1862, Butterfield revised a mournful bugle call—now played at nightfall in military posts, and at funerals—*Taps.*

101

The **Tattoo** signaled soldiers to stop carousing and return to their barracks.

A few hundred years ago armies used **two bugle calls** at the end of the day.

Butterfield hated *Lights Out.*

Summon the Brigade Bugler.

I cannot read music so I'll whistle a new tune and you will play it. This tune is called *Taps* and will **replace** *Lights Out.*

The next call—and actually the last call—was called **Lights Out** which meant "extinguish all fires and lights."

Butterfield's "tune" is *Taps* that is still sounded today.

There was a bugle call known as "To Extinguish Lights (or Taps)" in the U.S. Regulation Drum & Fife Instruction manual published in 1861 by Elias Howe. It was a take-off on a tattoo published in an 1836 army manual. Butterfield never claimed he composed *Taps.* Rather, he reworked the old music and made it more lyrical.

On July 2, 1862, at Harrison's Landing, VA, **Oliver Norton** of the 3rd Brigade, Morell's Division sounded *Taps* for the **first time**.

Taps quickly struck a popular note. The next day buglers from other units came to see Norton.

> Teach us that new call.

> Write down the notes.

Right after the bugler finished, a drummer would beat three taps; hence the bugle call was named *Taps*.

TAP TAP TAP

The first time that *Taps* was played at a funeral occurred late in July 1862 when a Union cannoneer was killed. It was the custom to fire a three-shot volley at a military burial, but the battery commander, Captain John Tidball, said....

> The shots might provoke the rebs to attack us...

Play that new bugle call... *Taps*.

The U.S. Army officially adopted *Taps* in 1874. Since 1900 *Taps* has been played at funerals of people who served in the Armed Forces of the United States.

103

While the big, critical battles were fought east of the Mississippi River, some little-known but important skirmishes took place in the west such as this incident in **New Mexico**.

The Fort Fillmore Fiasco

The South gave a high priority to **acquiring** the mineral-rich Territory of New Mexico which extended from Texas to California.

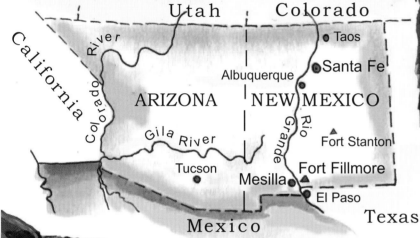

Realizing this Colonel Edward R. S. Canby, commander of the U.S. Department of New Mexico, transferred soldiers from outposts in Arizona to forts on the southeastern border of New Mexico to block any incursions by the Rebels moving in from Texas.

One such stronghold was **Fort Millard Fillmore** near the town of Mesilla, forty miles north of Confederate-held Fort Bliss at El Paso, Texas. **Major Isaac Lynde** commanded its garrison of 700 cavalry and infantry.

In late 1860 Colonel **John Robert Baylor**, a famous Texas lawyer, politician, and Indian fighter, advertised for 1,000 men to go on a "buffalo hunt." Actually he was recruiting a regiment of **Mounted Rifles**. By the start of the war in April 1861 he had a full compliment of 700 men. That summer they headed west to take over the deserted Federal outposts from Fort Lancaster to Fort Bliss at El Paso.

Along the way he left men to occupy each post, so when he reached Fort Bliss he had less than 400 men.

On July 23rd, 1861 he set out with about 250 to 300 men to spring a **surprise attack** on Fort Fillmore. Forewarned by pickets, Major Lynde put his men on full alert. Having lost the element of surprise, Baylor decided to hole up across the Rio Grande in Mesilla.

105

On July 25th, with superior numbers and confident of victory, Major Lynde led his forces out of the fort and marched to Mesilla.

He sent a man under a flag of truce into the town to demand the Texans surrender. Baylor refused. Lynde ordered his men to prepare to attack. Union howitzers fired a few shots which missed Baylor's men and only frightened some civilians who were walking up a nearby hill to watch the battle.

Lynde's cavalrymen lined up to charge, but as they advanced, one of Baylor's companies opened fire from their hidden positions alongside the road.

In a report he made later, Lynde said **three** of his 350 men were **killed** and six wounded by 700 Confederates. Baylor reported four of the enemy killed and eleven wounded, but he did not list any southern casualties.

The next day Major Lynde, without consulting his staff, decided to burn down the fort and march his force 154 miles across the desert to Fort Stanton.

Seeing the smoke on the horizon, Baylor quickly discerned Lynde's plan.

Mount up. Go after them!

Before leaving, a few hundred of Lynde's men filled their canteens with **whiskey** they stole from the hospital's storeroom.

The hard-riding Confederates soon caught up with the dehydrated, drunken stragglers who were quite happy to surrender.

Baylor's Mounties literally cut off Lynde's forces at the pass through the Organ Mountains. Although he had Baylor outnumbered by at least two to one, Lynde decided to surrender.

With that, Baylor captured the only significant Union force in the southern half of New Mexico.

107

The Confederate Territory of Arizona

By the end of 1861, Colonel J. R. Baylor and his Texas Mounties occupied all of the Union forts in New Mexico.

With the Yankees on the run, Baylor rode west to Tucson and took control of the federal garrisons in Arizona. He created the **Confederate Territory of Arizona.**

Baylor named himself governor, and the Confederate Congress confirmed his title. Declaring Mesilla, New Mexico as his capital, Baylor established a constitutional government in which all the key posts were held by his fellow Texans.

President Jefferson Davis made it official by issuing a proclamation on **February 14, 1862.** ✳

...(the) act to organize the **Territory of Arizona** (is now) in full force and operation.

Governor Baylor's major headache was the Mescalero Apaches. Ever since the northern forces evacuated, these Indians had been raiding the local ranches.

In March 1862 Baylor gave an unusual order to one of his officers.

"Invite all the Indians into your post for the purpose of making a treaty."

When they get there, **kill all the grown Indians** and take the children prisoners, then sell them to defray the expense of the killing.

In due time a copy of Baylor's order reached President Jefferson Davis.

Davis quickly fired Baylor.

Baylor left the army, went into politics, was elected to the Confederate House of Representatives from Texas in 1863, and served until the end of the war. He died in Montell, Texas, in 1894.

* Epilog—On **February 14, 1912**, exactly fifty years after Jefferson Davis created the Territory of Arizona, President William Howard **Taft** signed legislation making Arizona the **forty-eighth state.**

109

The Last Battle of the Civil War

The Confederate forces had surrendered by mid-April 1865 and the Federal War Department ordered its commanders to take control of state and local governments throughout the South.

The Confederates in Texas were aware of the surrender. Within days several hundred left the army and went home. But hundreds of others and their commanders stubbornly vowed to carry on the fight in Texas.

On May 11, Colonel Theodore Barrett, commander of a Union force on Brazos Island, Texas, sent Lt. Colonel Dave Branson and some 300 men, mostly African Americans, to move inland and take over the city of Brownsville.

At Palmito Ranch, twelve miles from Brownsville, the Yankees attacked 190 Confederate cavalrymen under the command of Captain George Roberson.

Roberson's men fell back and regrouped. The situation was shaping up to what became known as **the Battle of Palmito Ranch.**

The Federals, too, fell back to a hill overlooking the ranch to rest and cook dinner. Meanwhile Colonel "Rip" Ford had ordered Roberson to keep the pressure on the enemy and promised to send reinforcements as soon as possible. Feeling the pressure from the Texans, Lt. Col. Branson moved his Federals back about four miles to White's Ranch from where Branson sent a courier to Brazos Santiago asking his boss, Colonel Barrett, for reinforcements. Barrett arrived on May 13 with 200 men of the 34th Indiana Infantry, bringing the Union strength to 500 men.

Col. Barrett advanced his troops to Palmito Ranch and immediately attacked Roberson's 190 Confederates. At three in the afternoon Col. Ford arrived with 300 men from his own 2nd Texas Cavalry and Col. Santos Benavides's Texas Cavalry Regiment, plus a six-gun battery under Captain O. G. Jones. At 4 p.m Ford launched a counterattack. Having no artillery, Barrett ordered a retreat.

At 4 p.m. Jones's guns opened fire. When his artillery lifted (stopped), Roberson's men attacked the Union's left flank while Gidding's battalion hit the right. Ford's men charged the enemy center. Utterly surprised by this coordinated assault and without their own artillery, the Union forces fell back toward Brazos Island.

Colonel Barrett deployed 140 men of the 62nd Colored Infantry on a line from the Rio Grande to three quarters of a mile inland. They put up enough of a fight to delay the Confederates and allow the Federals to get away.

The 62nd Colored then retreated as the Confederates chased them for seven miles to Brazos Island. There the routed Yankees were reinforced, which prompted Colonel Ford to cease the attack.

Boys, we have done finely. We will let well enough alone and retire.

Ironically, on that very day the governors of Arkansas, Louisiana, Missouri, and Texas were ordering the abandonment of their armies to formally end the war.

A few days later, federal officers visited Brownsville to arrange a truce with General James Edwin Slaughter and Colonel Ford.

The Undefeated Rebel

General Joseph Orville Shelby, originally from Lexington, Kentucky, was the greatest **Missouri soldier** of the Confederacy. As a captain he took part in the famous Battle of Wilson Creek, Missouri, and made colonel after the Battle of Lone Jack, MO. He raised his own regiment which became known as the **Iron Brigade.**

From 1862 to 1863 he participated in attacks against Springfield and helped capture the federal strongholds at Neosho, Greenfield, Stockton, Booneville, Warsaw, and Hermanville, MO. During the autumn of 1864 his men took the railroad at Potosi, MO.

Shelby spent as much time fighting Confederate guerrillas as he did the Yankees in Missouri and Arkansas. Guerrillas were nothing more than thieves, terrorists, and killers operating under the guise of Confederate soldiers.

Shelby directed one of his battalion commanders, Lt. Colonel Joseph B. Love, "... shoot them (guerrillas) wherever found ... not one of them is to be spared."

General Joe Shelby and his Iron Brigade were stationed in Texas when the war ended. A month later, in May 1865, he addressed his troops from the porch of the Wyalucing Mansion in Marshall. He suggested they avoid becoming prisoners of war by fleeing to Mexico. His men liked the idea.

The Shelby Expedition added to the general confusion of postwar Texas as they traveled by way of Austin and San Antonio to Eagle Pass on the Rio Grande. Their conduct was no better than the guerrillas they had pursued during the war. They looted Confederate and state storehouses, seized food from farmers, and generally tore up the countryside.

The war ended with the collapse of the Confederacy as well as the governments of all its states. Governor Pendleton Murrah of Texas had skedaddled out of Austin to Mexico and there was no police force in the capital. On June 11, 1865, some looters broke into the treasury office and tried to haul off about $300,000.

Shelby's Iron Brigade was camped in Austin at the time. Some of his soldiers came to the rescue of the treasury, killed one of the looters, wounded several others, and drove off the rest of them. The looters got $1,700 for their troubles.

So, despite the havoc wreaked by Shelby's men on their trek across the state to Mexico, they did perform one good deed. They saved the state treasury from being looted completely.

116

Shelby's brigade resumed their expedition to Mexico. On crossing the Rio Grande, the general allowed his men to vote on whether they should offer their services to Juárez's patriots or to **Emperor Maximilian.** They chose Maximilian and proceeded to Mexico City, harassed all the way by attacks by Mexican guerrillas.

By the time Shelby's brigade had arrived in Mexico City, it had dwindled from several thousand to barely a thousand men ... and **Maximilian turned them down.** He did, however, grant them land to start the exile colony of Carlota (named after his wife, the empress) in the state of Vera Cruz. Some accepted his offer; others returned home. General Shelby stayed near the Carlota colony running a wagon freight company.

The French Army went back to Europe in 1867 leaving Maximilian with only loyal Mexican and Indian soldiers to ward off Juárez and his revolutionaries. The emperor was ultimately defeated at Querétaro and later executed.

Without the protection of Maximilian, Shelby and the Confederate colonists were constantly hassled by the revolutionaries. Shelby returned to Missouri in the summer of 1867. He began growing wheat near Lexington, and invested in railroads and coal mines.

In 1893 he was appointed **U.S. Marshal** of the Western District of Missouri, a job he held until his death in 1897.

Bibliography

Bakeless, John. *Spies of the Confederacy.* Mineola, NY: Dover Publications, 1970.

Baker, Lafayette. *History of the U. S. Secret Service.* Philadelphia, PA: L. C. Baker, 1867.

Barrow, Charles Kelly, J. H. Segars, and R. B. Rosenburg. *Black Confederates.* Gretna, LA: Pelican, 1995.

Bragdon, Henry W. and Samuel P. McCutchen. *History of a FreePeople.* New York: Macmillan, 1958.

Brant, Nat. *The Man Who Tried to Burn New York.* Syracuse, NY: Syracuse University Press, 1986.

Bruce, R. *Lincoln and the Tools of War.* Indianapolis, IN: Bobbs-Merrill, 1956.

Chase, Gilbert. *America's Music From the Pilgrims to the Present.* Urbana and Chicago, IL: University of Illinois Press, 1987.

Colton, Ray C. *The Civil War in the Western Territories.* Norman, OK: University of Oklahoma Press, 1959.

Cottom, Robert I, Jr. and Mary Ellen Hayward. *Maryland in the Civil War.* Baltimore, MD: Maryland Historical Society, 1994.

Cottrell, Steve. *Civil War in Texas and New Mexico Territory.* Gretna, LA: Pelican, 1998.

Davis, Kenneth. *Don't Know Much About the Civil War* New York: Avon, 1996.

Dietz, August. *The Postal Service of the Confederate States of America.* Richmond, VA: Press of the Dietz Printing Co., 1929.

District of Columbia History Curriculum Project. *City of Magnificent Intentions—A History of the District of Columbia.* Washington, DC: Associates for Renewal in Education, 1983.

Frank Leslie's Illustrated Newspaper. May 18, 1861.

Henson, Michael Paul. *Guide to Treasure in Pennsylvania.* Conroe, TX: True Treasure Library, 1977.

Hessler, Ken. *Legendary 'Old Abe" Still Soars With Eagles.* Fort Campbell, KY: Public Affairs Committee Special Report, 101st Airborne Division Assn., 2006.

Hyson, John M., Jr. and Margaret Requa DeFrancisco. *Dr. Joseph Requa Civil War Dentist and the Billinghurst-Requa Volley Gun.* Alexandria Bay, NY: Museum Restoration Service, 1998.

Jordan, Evrin L., Jr. *Black Confederates and Afro-Yankees in Civil War Virginia.* Charlottesville, VA: University Press of Virginia, 1995.

Junior League of Washington. *An Illustrated History of the City of Washington.* New York: Alfred A. Knopf, 1985.

Kuff, Karen R.. *Gold in Maryland.* Baltimore: Maryland Geological Survey Pamphlet Series, 1987.

Lossing, Benson J. *Pictorial Field Book of the Civil War.* Baltimore and London: Johns Hopkins University Press, 1997.

Markle, Donald E. *Spies and Spymasters of the Civil War.* New York: Hippocrene, 1994.

McHenry, Robert. *Famous American Women.* New York: Dover, 1980.

McKay, Ernest A. *The Civil War in New York City.* Syracuse, NY: Syracuse University Press, 1990.

New Handbook of Texas, Austin, TX: The Texas State Historical Association, 1996.

Peters, James Edward. *Arlington National Cemetery-Shrine to America's Heroes.* Kensington, MD: Woodbine House, 1986.

Shephard, Sue. *Pickled, Potted, and Canned.* New York: Simon and Schuster, 2000.

Sifakis, Stewart. *Who Was Who in the Civil War.* New York: Facts on File, 1988.

Tucker, Philip T.. *From Auction Block to Glory.* New York: Metrobooks, 1998.

Wallace, Irving, David Wassechinsky, and Amy Wallace. *Significa.* New York, E. P. Dutton, 1983.

Wideman, John C. *Naval Warfare-Courage and Combat on the Water.* New York: Metrobooks, 1997.

Index

120

121

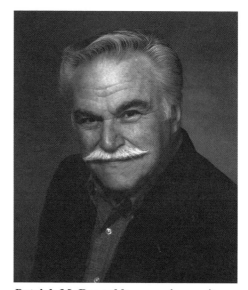

Patrick M. Reynolds researches, writes, and illustrates *Flashbacks* which appears every Sunday in the *Washington Post* and other newspapers. His series of illustrated history books include: *Pennsylvania Profiles, Big Apple Almanac, Texas Lore, A Cartoon History of the District of Columbia,* and *A Cartoon History of Texas.* In the Vietnam War he served as a Military Intelligence Officer. A Lt. Colonel, he taught military history and tactics at the U.S. Army Command and General Staff Officers Course. He and his wife Patricia live in the town of Willow Street, Pennsylvania.